Sagebrush Songs

poems by

Margaret Lee

Finishing Line Press
Georgetown, Kentucky

Sagebrush Songs

For Brandon,
desert companion

Copyright © 2022 by Margaret Lee
ISBN 978-1-64662-756-1 First Edition
All rights reserved under International and Pan-American Copyright Conventions. No part of this book may be reproduced in any manner whatsoever without written permission from the publisher, except in the case of brief quotations embodied in critical articles and reviews.

ACKNOWLEDGMENTS

An earlier version of "Into the Desert" appears as "Desert Yearning" in *Someone Else's Earth*, (Finishing Line Press, 2021).

Publisher: Leah Huete de Maines
Editor: Christen Kincaid
Cover Art: Margaret Lee
Author Photo: Bernard B. Scott
Cover Design: Elizabeth Maines McCleavy

Order online: www.finishinglinepress.com
also available on amazon.com

Author inquiries and mail orders:
Finishing Line Press
PO Box 1626
Georgetown, Kentucky 40324
USA

Table of Contents

Poems and Landscape 1

Into the Desert
Into the Desert 3
Nowhere to Run 4
Canyon Plumb Line 5
Desert Extravagance 7
Lifeways 8
Storm on the Taos Plateau 9
Coyote Vision 10

Winter
Hatchling Day 11
Snowbirds 12
Snowscape 13
The Living Snow 14
Frost Journey 15
Sufficiency 16

Mountain Murmurs
Why? 17
Clouds at Taos Mountain 19
The Golden Cities 20
The Great Rift 22
Near Chama 23
At Echo Amphitheater 24
Bewitched 26
Geophagy 27

Sagebrush Songs
Stillness Stirs 28
Song at the Rio Hondo 29
Confluence 30
The Hum 31
Afternoon in the Enchanted Circle 32
Sagebrush Songs 33

Poems and Landscape

Sagebrush Songs arises from the northern New Mexico landscape, remote and unique. The headwaters of the Rio Grande and one of its major tributaries, the Rio Chama, originate in the southern Rocky Mountains. A high desert plateau stretches between the Tusas and Sangre de Christo ranges in this mountain system. The Rio Grande rift, a major continental rift zone, runs through the plateau. As a transitional zone between alpine forests and shortgrass prairie, the sagebrush mesa supports diverse animal and plant communities. A scenic roadway around Wheeler Peak, the highest point in New Mexico, defines the Enchanted Circle a few miles north of the Taos Pueblo. Pueblo Peak, popularly known as Taos Mountain, is revered because the Taos Pueblo's water supply originates there, and because of the mountain's striking contour in the Sangre de Christo range.

The ancient Chinese understanding of *Tao* sees mountains and rivers as expressions of yin and yang, the energies that animate fundamental creative material. *Tao*, or "the Way," contemplates mountains and rivers in terms of processes that continually generate and regenerate all things as they emerge from and recede into empty absence. Classical Chinese poetry meditates on such landscape features and their empty spaces. Learning to be present in northern New Mexico enables me to understand why this is so. *Sagebrush Songs* is my meditation on its mountains and rivers as manifestations of the Way of all things.

Into the Desert

Into the Desert

Abandon me to the desert
    with chamisa and sage
where only ants
    and armored beetles crawl
where lizards skitter
    from shadows among the rocks
where rabbit and raven
    patrol earth and sky.

The endless wind travels there alone—
    now subtle, now rumbling with pressure—
the earth's breath undulating with change
    the coming and going of days
retreating summer, advancing winter
    spasms of storm.

Let there be moonlight, always in motion—
    first a glow from behind mountain peaks
then bright beams across the steppe
    casting shadows—
flashlights exposing, then eclipsing
    every minor mound, each tiny crack—
making arroyos yawn, gape,
    then disappear—
proving the desert surface remains,
    arid and spare, even in the dark.

Nowhere to Run

Where water is scarce
high-desert plants
spread their roots
drop them deeper
hang on, reaching
for distant water.
They neither shrink nor fade.
What drives the impulse
to lean into danger
resist it, withstand it,
adapt?

To survive in saline soil
greasewood and saltbush
drink it up
store the salt in their pith
becoming saltier
than the groundwater,
enabling osmosis.
Thus they thrive.

Yesterday I found
the crisp remains
of a sunflower three feet tall.
It had sent out green leaves
and bright blossoms
then scattered its seeds—
its base surrounded
by asphalt.

Canyon Plumb Line

Canyon-wall pillars drop roots—
trace time's passage
from when this rock, still liquid
still embedded in magma,
river gravel, or ash—
always in motion—
had yet to live
in the shape we see it now.

The time it takes
the earth to form
to crack in precise patterns
to shed its scree and show its shape
to stand for a while
until the earth gets its bearings
then moves again—

That time began
thousands and millions of years ago
before anyone knew what a year was—
before anyone existed, before knowing—
when fossil-creatures evolved.
Whole empires have come and gone
since then.

The path we walk, the rock we see
ride time's slow continuum.
Still she moves, our churning Earth.
When she shrugs her shoulders
the mountains lift higher.
She stretches her legs
and the plain reaches
farther west.

So the rift gapes
and water soothes the wound—
drops deep to where the surface splits
and edges retreat.
Cool liquor runs to the sea, its home—
carries sandy, gravel memories
of another place, another time.

Desert Extravagance

The summer monsoon
strews wildflower jewels
across the desert
into river gorges—
cholla cactus, lupine,
milkvetch, larkspur, thistle,
yellow sweet clover.
Then, with autumn's advent
their colors drain
from the shrubland
sowing seeds latent
with next year's display
leaving grey-green sagebrush plains
adorned with occasional asters—
tiny purple stars
that preserve a memory
of summer's desert blooms.

Lifeways

I hear car tires grind desert dirt
and know the road remains
unharmed.

sagebrush contorts its shape, twists
around fugitive water,
light.

piñons bend their branches, trunks—
wait through bleak years to yield
rich nuts.

the desert wears its scars, the marks
of scarcity, no fear
of change.

Storm on the Taos Plateau

Bundles of mist gather, curl
        suspended aloft on
        an invisible plate
twisting around a stormy center—
a cloud-lariat reining in
        the clash
        the lightning flash.

Blue-grey rain-streaks
        from the spreading center
        connect heaven and earth—
sharp edges blur
a rush of pressure
        the thrust—
        rain spreads like dust.

Coyote Vision

Awake under a near-full moon
I remember the clear-eyed coyote

in daylight at the instant
our sightlines crossed.

We both stopped, watching
each other in our places, focused

as if under moonlight, knowing
our connection in that moment—

then resumed our different paths
changed but unchanged.

Winter

Hatchling Day

Morning light in eggshell tones—
a thin ribbon reaching around
this high plateau horizon
against the mountain-range silhouette—
pale light leaves the sky's expanse
dense with smoke-grey cloud.

Not bright enough yet
to expose the source
of squeaking sounds arising
from the inches between
low sagebrush branches
and drought-hardened earth.
Perhaps a sage thrasher chasing
a needle-legged spider
or a striped chipmunk fleeing
a coyote's scent.

Darting movement peppers the ground
in the swift stretch of growing light
along the rocky surface
between clumps
of sage and chamisa.

Snowbirds

This morning the juncos perch
in juniper shrubs, on the sagebrush.

Avoiding the snow-covered ground
they feed on silver-green branches.

Crisp and sharp against the snow, their black heads
frame pink beaks and cloak burnt-orange flanks.

The snow erases their camouflage, brings them close.
Colors clear now, their shapes puffed out

they stand distinct from white-crowned sparrows
and strawberry-headed house finches.

Because of this, fear cannot exist—because
the birds, the snow, their patterns, change.

Snowscape

Snow-mound
contours mirror
cloud-cloaked mountain peaks in
icy orogeny. Ranges
of drifts

transform
the sagebrush plain,
obscure its floor, fill its
fissures. Earth, sky, churn lavender
and grey.

The Living Snow

Falling, the snow-creature's birth begins.
It flies with heavy blue wings, cranes its neck.

Falling flakes disguise the snow as a particle cloud
while the looming chimera descends, noiseless.

Shifting shapes mutate, spill into mounds,
form ice crusts, reshape underlying surfaces

shifting identities. The snow-being contorts its drift-tentacles,
clings to the shade, raises earth's floor with hollow depths.

Melting mounds compress their mass. Silent rivulets descend,
run deep beneath shimmering sun-touched surfaces.

Melting masses slouch, doubled by their shadows
as the snow-being writhes, shrinks, retreats to the horizon.

Frost Journey

Vapor ascends, invisible,
from desert mesa
snow-shapes.

Snagged by sagebrush branches
it freezes in the cold dark—
becomes at sunrise
a fleeting, crystalline gleam

reflecting, with diamond-studded drifts,
clear, mountain light
beneath a glassy sky.

Sufficiency

The light
at dawn, changing—
screened by mountains, filtered
by clouds, melting snow—the scaled quail
come, gone.

Mountain Murmurs

Why?

Because there is less—
that is the whole reason.
Less air, less water.
One must choose.
Assign priorities.
Little can be sustained.
What you have
is what you carry
into the desert
or what you eke out
of dried arroyos, sunbaked earth.
What you do not need
the thin air washes away
in floods of sunlight.

I go because the silent mountains,
their pine-covered curves—
violet-blue in the morning
reddened in evening light—
stand as sole authority
a magnetic orientation
a stony history
of earth's folding and faulting
volcanic violence
glacial grinding
weary erosion.
I go because their peaks, still rising,
stare down into the Great Rift,
Earth's unresolved unease—
a gash gouged all the way to the sea.

Less to do, to distract—
one's self clearly delimited—
simpler, more factual
closer to life's boundary
closer to actual size.

Clouds at Taos Mountain

Soft, grey arms—
their gathering embrace
of the blue peak,
light beyond—
so slow they recalibrate
the clock.

Dawn nods her pink yes
then leaves the clouds
to their large migration.
Sagebrush sundials
register the change.
Heavy moisture masses—
spa sponges—
trace the contours
of Earth's skin.

The Golden Cities

Had he come in October
Coronado would have found
his sparkling Cities of Cibola.
With autumn's advent
high-altitude sunlight
stirs the cool, mountain air
draining onto the Taos plateau.
Then the elusive gold
erupts across hillside and mesa.

White-trunked aspen infuse mountain forests
that rise like cathedral walls, lofty, sacred,
blanketed in deepest green
like darkness itself.
The aspen's leafy columns
flare like candles
among the evergreens
blazing and brilliant
intensifying daylight.

Stream bed bosques glow
with golden-leaved cottonwoods
peachleaf willows, and locust trees—
shimmering gold drapery
along the riverbanks.
The broad plateau
effervesces with chamisa.
Their golden froth
spreads like prairie fire
along roadways and arroyos
where scarce water runs.

A double-ringed boundary—
the Enchanted Circle and the Taos plateau—
surrounds the golden cities
that spread riches
overhead and underfoot,
burnished in mountain rafters, on canyon walls,
in gold-paved desert streets—
elusive, enduring
Cities of Gold.

The Great Rift

Although
earth's skin appears
firm, stable, solid, fixed,
its rocks move, bending and folding—
alive.

Beneath
shifting layers,
steamy magma churning,
volcanoes ignite, mountains rise,
earth cracks.

East, west
divide, retreat,
break open a great rift
between mountain heights and desert
plateau.

Running
cold, a river
traces the canyon floor.
The deep, broken earth understands
its course.

Mountains
keep pulling east,
rising, blocking the sun,
while the plain recedes to the west,
its fate.

Although
shifting layers
break open a great rift,
the deep, broken earth understands
its fate.

Near Chama

The postcard caption
stops short.
Every place is near Chama
if your scale is right.
I'm near enough
to get there in one day.
No need for a map.
Pursue the scent of sagebrush
then head further west.
Ascend 10,000 feet.
Follow the cold air
heavy with pine.
You will be alone.
That's why you should go.

At Echo Amphitheater

The cliff face
along the edge
of the Colorado Plateau
ranges on for miles
in New Mexico—
just east of the lands
allotted to the Ute, Navajo,
and Jicarilla Apache nations.
Beneath the plateau's crust
with its surface fuzz
of piñon and sage,
rocky strata register
the passage of geologic time
in sandstone layers
of cinnamon and saffron
and a layer the color of storm clouds.

On the west side of Highway 84,
ten miles north of where
they dammed the Rio Chama,
the cliff hollows out
a massive dome.
Echo Amphitheater yawns
where the ground percolates with
rabbits and towhees,
where spiders and snakes
enact their ancient dramas
against a backdrop of juniper
and prickly pear.

Human dramas unfold there, too,
luring hikers into the bowl,
back, back,
uphill half a mile
to the canyon wall.

Many respect the silence,
stare in awe
at the sheer expanse
spreading wide and deep.
Others test the famous echo
and laugh.
But the twisted pines
and stunted scrub oaks
that crawl like crabbed handwriting
deep into the theater
hide darker deeds.
Brown streaks
run from the rocky rim,
falling like tears
down the concave wall—
bloodstains
from murder and retribution
where the red and white strata
of human skin colors
clashed.

Or so they say.
Memories of violence
and mysteries of vitality
mix in the amphitheater
with the chattering of canyon wrens
and the reverberating breeze.
A sacred hush prevails,
like a church
with its stony floor
and pillars all around the rim
standing still,
shoulder to shoulder,
like ancient ancestors,
watching.

Bewitched

Halloween glowers,
lurks around the corner
as the Luna fire pours smoke
onto the Taos plateau.
In the dead of night
the Sangre de Christos glow red with flame
in a macabre perversion of their name.
Flaring, surging, the fire
rages with churning heat
like an infected wound.

At daybreak,
as the sun clears Pueblo Peak
the light is almost too bright,
reflected by the haze
into a blinding glare so dense
it eclipses the fire.
Smoke phantoms
transform the view
across turquoise skies.
Clouds look like mountains,
smoke looks like clouds,
dry haze looks like rain,
the very air confused,
deceived.

Note:
The Luna Fire broke out on October 17, 2020, two miles north of Chacon, New Mexico, in the Carson National Forest. It burned for nearly a month before it was contained.
https://inciweb.nwcg.gov/incident/7246/

Geophagy

On sagebrush hills in Chimayó,
people once ate the earth,
sprinkled its red grit on their heads,
rubbed it into their skin.
They still do.

I think I understand.
Thin soil nourishes the ancient
Three Sisters: beans, squash, corn.
Nearby rocks yield silver, turquoise.
Kilns gestate earthen pots
carved with snake designs,
encircled by feather motifs,
adorned with patterns
that repeat the undulation
of surrounding volcanic peaks.
Of course the earth is sacred.
Her travelled grains
with chemical knowledge
and magnetic pull
support us,
comprise us,
consume us
after death.

I, too, yearn to drink the earth
and its mystery—
to cover myself in its colors,
bury myself in its warmth,
absorb its secrets,
feel its power.

Sagebrush Songs

Stillness Stirs

What song
reverberates
from this desert-basin
singing bowl as the mountain rim,
wind-whipped,

light-stroked,
vibrates with breeze,
brushes the starry dome,
sends hymns through arid plains, creekside
bosques?

It sings.
Who hears? Ravens,
rabbits, a coyote?
The moonlit, sagebrush silence waits,
listens.

Song at the Rio Hondo

I saw him at the canyon rim, sitting
on a camp chair near his car as I drove past.

Head bowed, he embraced a guitar
And sang to the river, the pines, the melting snow.

His strum reverberated through the rocks
like echoes of seismic vibrations, canyon winds.

Did he sing of ancient longing, or loss, or loved ones
now distant, like the stream at the canyon floor?

Deep River, they call it, *Rio Hondo,* tracing a crack
in the earth, holding its mysteries, at home in its depths.

Confluence

Descending the Arroyo Hondo
      sharp shadows shift
            over pillared rocks—
    sun-stabs
into gorge depths.

I crest the canyon rim
      descend dusty switchbacks—
          yes, I hear it now—
    water catchment—
clear, cold

under a canopy of coneflowers,
      cholla, cow parsnip.
           The stream pursues
  a slim river running
beyond the bridge.

The Hum

Never still.
Daylight and starlight,
the sage-streaked breeze,
the canyons and their river bosques,
the scent of piñon pine
oscillate around a center,
and the center sings
the song of being
with all that is.

I am that song
that persists, pervades,
glows and fades.
Its rhythms and rests,
harmonies and dissonances
attuned to all that is.

Afternoon in the Enchanted Circle

Standing between me
and the rest—
attention, seeing—
popcorn thoughts.

When unattended
they switch off
like a computer screen
going black.

They are impatient.
I am patient. I wait.
Thoughts sleep,
I awaken.

Then it's all there—
the lizard, the thistle
the hummingbird
the scent of sage.

A birdcall, just behind,
just beneath the song
of the house finch—
Eurasian collared dove?

Is that why they make
cedar flutes, to play
that haunting song? To join
that winged lament?

Sagebrush Songs

Sagebrush
songs, lavender
and light, the incense from
smoky piñon fires—the desert
beckons.

With Thanks

Many thanks to Leah Maines, Kevin Maines, and Christen Kincaid of Finishing Line Press for editorial support, and to editorial assistants Jackie Steelman and Elizabeth Maines McCleavy for their attention to detail in copyediting and design. The annual Poetry Postcard Fest, sponsored by the Cascadia Poetics Lab (formerly the Seattle Poetics Lab), furnished the occasion for an early draft of "Near Chama." Caroline Davies wrote a lovely response to that poem on a postcard she sent to me during the 2021 Fest. Jan Smith and SOMOS (the Society of the Muse of the Southwest) have enriched my poetry pursuits with online workshops, the SOMOS bookstore in Taos, and the annual Taos Writers Conference. I owe my gratitude to many who have encouraged my journey as a poet. These include especially Rick and Amber Dean, Ginny Eckley, Judy Nill, James Gaynor, and Lorelei Sanchez. Susan Roberts befriends me honestly enough to observe that creating both the poems and the cover art for a poetry chapbook is "just showing off." Brandon Scott has shared my desert journeys with an intimacy spacious enough to accommodate both adventure and solitude.

Margaret Lee is retired as Assistant Professor of Humanities at Tulsa Community College in Tulsa, Oklahoma. She attended Edgecliff College in Cincinnati, Ohio and graduated with a Bachelor of Arts in History from Seattle University in Seattle, Washington. She received a Master of Divinity from Phillips Theological Seminary in Tulsa, Oklahoma, and a Doctor of Theology from the Melbourne College of Divinity in Melbourne, Australia. Her doctoral dissertation, *A Method for Sound Analysis in Hellenistic Greek*, proposes a process for analyzing ancient Greek literature as speech. She is the editor of *Sound Matters: New Testament Studies in Sound Mapping* (Eugene, OR: Wipf and Stock, 2018) and is co-author with Bernard Brandon Scott of *Sound Mapping the New Testament* (Salem, OR: Polebridge Press, 2009). Margaret has written numerous articles on the Greek language and New Testament studies in edited books and peer-reviewed academic journals.

Before teaching the Humanities to undergraduates, Margaret spent six years working in the finance industry in Seattle, Washington, then twenty-five years in higher education administration in Tulsa, Oklahoma. She raised her daughter and son in Tulsa and now has three grandchildren. Margaret avidly pursues the fiber arts, including spinning, weaving, and knitting. Margaret enjoys sketching with pencil, ink, and watercolor. She is an enthusiastic birdwatcher and aspiring naturalist. Margaret loves exploring the Oklahoma prairies, New Mexico deserts, and Oregon coastal forests and seashores. She is a member of the Society of Biblical Literature, a fellow of the Westar Institute, an officer of the Tulsa Handspinner's Guild, and past president of the Tulsa Handweavers Guild. Margaret is a member of the Tulsa NightWriters, the Oklahoma Writers Federation, Inc., the Society of the Muse of the Southwest (SOMOS), and the Academy of American Poets.

www.ingramcontent.com/pod-product-compliance
Lightning Source LLC
LaVergne TN
LVHW041603070426
835507LV00011B/1284